Looking for Ideas?

A Display Manual
for Libraries and Bookstores

by

Clair H. Wallick

The Scarecrow Press, Inc.
Metuchen, N. J.   1970

PHOTOGRAPHS

by

Chester E. Pancoast

BETTY   PEARL   MILDRED

Dedicated

to

MY THREE GRACES

Thalis. . . . .   Betty

Aglaia. . . . .   Pearl

Euphrosyne . . . . Mildred

The Author

Preface

You never know exactly when an idea for a book crystalizes and pushes itself to the fore. Perhaps I have always had a vague feeling that "someday I'm going to . . ." or maybe the day Grace Walker, my immediate supervisor, said, "What a shame all your efforts will be for such a short time," the concept began. Somewhere between these two ideas the possibility of preserving my ideas in a book became a reality.

I gathered together the numerous books we have in our collection and tried to find examples of my thoughts on the subject of window displays featuring books.

There were none. This was the deciding factor.

I hope the following text and illustrations help you with your display designing. The basic element that is needed is you--you and your determined interest in producing a finished display which fulfills your desired results and sense of self-accomplishment.

I could prattle on indefinitely about commercial supply sources, provide lists and lists of free material sources, et cetera, but this is not my purpose. I want to give you ideas that will start you thinking and creating along the lines of display work. I want to plant a seed, not tell you of my harvest.

At this moment you have everything needed within reach. I hope to convince you of this fact. If I do, then my efforts will be preserved--for a longer time than I had expected.

Clair Wallick

Montgomery County - Norristown Public Library
Norristown, Pennsylvania

CONTENTS

Preface

x

Me, A Display Designer?

The years have been kind; good schooling, above average grades, graduation and finally you are the proud possessor of a degree. You have decided the world of books is for you. This may lead you into retailing or perchance to the vocation of a librarian.

You find the job most suitable to you--in a wage bracket you like, no less--and all seemingly is going well. Then one day the display area becomes your responsibility. Me, a display designer? Why I never. . . . But the responsibility remains in your bailiwick and that gaping monster of empty space looms before you. You wonder if your services are needed in Tanganyika.

But before you buy that one way ticket let us take a firm grip on the situation and see what we can develop. The problems involved in producing a good display are not that difficult. Time, effort, materials, and imagination are the major requirements. Are you really lacking any of these? No, of course not. You know you aren't. So let us examine in detail their various sources and the possible uses to which we can put them.

No Time Trauma and the Effortless Effort Excuse

The first two requirements of time and effort we quite often obliterate by the self induced No Time Trauma and the Effortless Effort Excuse; the combination of both being analyzed as Let's Forget the Whole Thing. Isn't it astonishing how many other things seem to continuously occupy your time? The workday is already overflowing? Not enough hours? Another report due tomorrow? Board meeting coming up?

Enough! Enough!

Alloting time to work on your display is not difficult once you establish the habit. First of all you must decide you want to take the time. Even if you start out with only an hour, it is an hour you were not devoting to design last week. After your ideas and materials are organized (to be discussed) the actual construction time can be fairly well predicted. As your enthusiasm increases and favorable comments build confidence, so will construction time take priority.

The Effortless Effort Excuse can be abolished once you realize that your attitude--that anyone can do a display--is merely blasé defensiveness. What at first seems to be an endless effort to start and complete a display project will in time turn itself into unlimited energy and enthusiasm. But this, too, is related to the self confidence that comes with continuous participation.

The idea of beginning your first display may paralyze you at first but you're no different from the actor appearing on stage for the first time (and many times thereafter), the prize fighter entering the ring (yes, even the favorite can have his moments of doubt) or, remembering back, your feelings when settling down to final exams (which were passed successfully). There will usually be the need to prod yourself so that the No Time Trauma and Effortless Effort Excuse do not become your constant companions.

Let them keep company together. They deserve each other, not you.

Imagine That!

How many dreary times have you heard someone say, or you yourself said (to yourself I hope), "If only I could do that?" How many times has this statement been applied to simple, everyday events or functions? True, we all can't walk in space yet, but give us time. There are, however, many things to which we can apply ourselves and our imagination and come up with some fine results. This strongly applies to the displays that may still seem to be an albatross around your neck.

First think of a theme. Halloween? Fine! Now, how do you go about turning this into a display that is out of the ordinary? Something that has your stamp of individuality on it? Let's do a little free associating as our psychiatrists are always telling us to do.

Halloween? Halloween! Pumpkins . . . October . . . ghosts . . . trick or treat . . . black cats . . . skeletons . . . graveyards . . . graveyards!

Ah, here is a possibility. But how do you create and capture the essence of your graveyard within the confines of your display area? Cardboard skeletons? Paper ghosts and tombstones? It has been done. A real tombstone? Yes! Why not? What else? Keep going now that you've started so well. Dead leaves. A gnarled branch. Old rusty chains. A few plastic spiders. Yes, yes! Great imagination.

See, it simply comes down to trying to place basic, everyday events, whether it be a holiday, election, or return to school theme, in a one-of-a-kind, not-done-before setting. Only your imagination need be invested to take you out of your Paper Pumpkin Period (in regard to Halloween). Just imagine what you can do with the rest of the year of events.

Now let's assume you have a setting: a complete, detailed picture of just what you want to create. How many

16

themes could be used with this one setting? You have a wonderful, white winterscape in mind: piles of artificial snow, evergreen branches, cool blue backdrops and a mirrored lake completes the picture.

What theme will be the most unique?

You could use winter sports or bird feeding in winter. Even a promotion for books on the Nordic countries is good. But suppose you were to use this display in July or August? Toss in a few books such as Winter's Tale, Ice Palace, et cetera, and a sign reading "Beat the Heat" or "Cool It. " Is anyone passing by likely not to stop? Winter in summer. The visual effect is almost better than air conditioning. For a moment or two, winter is in the viewer's mind and the surrounding summer heat is vanquished. Instant escapism.

Your original thinking can really produce some superb results. The most important one to be obtained, besides the unique displays, will be your complete satisfaction.

Imagine that!

4

"Gather Ye . . ."

Display budgets are always a problem, namely because
of their size--minute--but except for a few basics such as
paper, paints, glue, scissors, et cetera, most of your materials can be obtained for practically no cost at all. Again
the one element needed is you and, this time, your constant
searching.

While visiting the seashore or mountains notice the
abundance of nature's wonderful materials with which to form
and frame your displays. Even your own locale is brimming
over with these gifts. Your local stone-cutter can provide
you with that tombstone we conjured up in the last chapter.
What is to prevent you from taking a short trip to your local
athletic goods store to borrow some equipment for a sports
promotion?

Or a local antique dealer will more than welcome the
advertising space you will provide by using his merchandise
in a creative way for a few weeks. The only expense involved is merely a small card included in your display which
reads, ". . . through the courtesy of . . ."

Donations can be an excellent source of your materials.
Merchants often receive standard displays which they may use
for a short time and then discard. Check this possible source
out. You may not want to use the whole display intact (hopefully, if you intend to use any of your own creativity) but
some part or parts of it will surely prove useful. Local
organizations, clubs and individual collectors provide another
source of free materials. They, too, are pleased to have
their particular interests or possessions exhibited. Remember,
they cherish their mementos or collections and are usually
most willing to share with the public. Again, the price to
be paid is only the courtesy card included in the display.

And there are always those things you can "borrow"
from yourself. Take inventory of your own private stock.

18

Lamps, pictures, objets d'art that you own certainly can fill in successfully when needed.

The important factor is to constantly be aware of possible sources and resources. This takes practice but a searching eye and mind can be developed. It's not unlike Christmas shopping on a fifty-two week basis. In time this seeking becomes an unconscious habit and you will be constantly scanning for new possibilities.

When you do see these materials that hold interesting ideas for you, try to obtain them then and there. If you put off acquiring them, the chances of your coming back or their being there when they are needed are slim. Very slim, indeed.

"Gather ye . . . while ye may . . ."

5

Organize! Organize!

We all realize organizing is a must if anything is to be accomplished within a reasonable length of time and with any degree of efficiency. Whether it is a vacation, report or display you want to prepare you must organize your plans. This does not preclude your chasing the will-of-the-wisps when new ideas occur. The more ideas that are considered the greater the selection will be when you need to create one in a material form. But when an idea is selected as your next project then it is time to concentrate. Agreed? Good!

The subject is selected. What materials are needed? How is this to be laid out? Is there a definite color scheme to follow? Where can you find the objects still needed for your plan? What is the selection of books to be used? How much time will be entailed to complete the entire display?

Hopefully your previously gathered treasures (you have been gathering, haven't you?) will yield some help. Either sketch or diagram the completed display you envision. This is a great aid in scaling and placing the objects being used. That lamp or bowl may not be just the right size when placed in the display. Carefully scale in advance. It helps eliminate those frantic, last minute changes.

What colors will predominate? If possible it is best to use a coordinated color scheme. Granted, books are not being printed in colors you specify but if the rest of the display has color unity, the books used can only be that much more outstanding. Sometimes if only one book is being featured, the colors can be picked up from the jacket.

In one instance a local publisher was collaborating with us on a display featuring their products. We used their trademark colors of green and gold for the background. It identified our subject and enhanced the books being used.

One of the best aids in organizing your display is to complete a dummy set up before the actual installation for your public. From this you can judge, change, add, or eliminate. Also the actual installation time is shortened since you know exactly where every item is to be placed. This is an excellent aid.

You have probably deduced by now that once your theme is definite, the time for daydreaming is over. Efficiency becomes your guide. Having finished and installed your display (to the ohs and ahs of passersby) then it is time for you to wander among the clouds and pick another shining star.

"The World of Books"

is the most remarkable creation of man;
nothing else . . . ever lasts . . . nations
perish . . . new races build others . . .
books . . . live on . . . still telling men's
hearts of the hearts of men centuries dead.

Clarence Day

This entire display is centered around the ideas ex-
pressed above. A selection of books ranging from Homer
to Shakespeare to Salinger are used to illustrate the perma-
nency books have in men's lives. The accessories are
selected (borrowed from the author's own miscellaneous
memorabilia) with the idea of covering man's thoughts from
ancient Greece to contemporary Giacometti.

The materials used are of no cost except for the few
yards of black and white check fabric used as a simulated
wallpaper background. (Fabric is easier to handle, usually
has a good strong color, and can be less expensive than
wallpaper of the same quality. Check your mill-end stores.)

Here, books are incorporated into the display as a
natural part of the background and are used to illustrate the
overall theme instead of being featured--an indirect approach
to "the world of books" with a very direct message to your
viewers.

The complete text by Clarence Day is used as one of
the pictures hanging on the wall.

U F O ?

A subject of current interest--unidentified flying objects--forms the basis for this interesting display.

Only a few yards of leftover Christmas snow paper are required to create our unknown planet's terrain. A piece of plywood stained with peacock blue ink to accent the graining provides the background of eerie air currents and vapor patterns. The UFO's in the background are the knot plugs in the plywood and are painted a pale blue. Our two large UFO's are inverted ceiling light globes found on the discard pile in the basement. Inside, blinking lights send out undeciphered messages. Unfortunately, the amber acetate windows do not permit us to see the inhabitants.

A definite color scheme is used of blue, white and amber. Since only one book is used, its cover being blue, our color coordination is completely controlled. Another advantage of using only one book in a display is that it frees all other books available on the subject matter for circulation.

So by using only leftovers and discards we have again piqued our public.

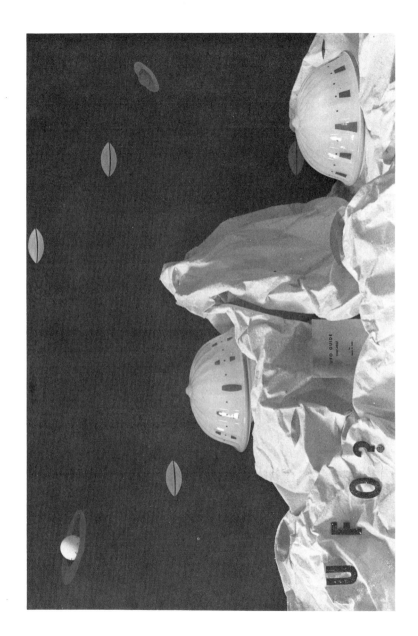

Sports

By using a pale blue background on which a red and white brick wall has been stenciled we begin our display on sports. The foreground is covered with a bed of white pebbles that is a part of our previously gathered materials.

All of the athletic equipment is borrowed from our local sporting goods store and we have appropriately included our courtesy card giving credit to our lender.

This is an extremely simple and inexpensive display to create. Imaginative placement of the equipment must be used or else it can easily turn into a chaotic assemblage. Wherever possible the pieces are suspended with clear nylon fishing line, e. g. , tennis racket, book and ball. The arrow is balanced on the three supporting shafts. Through these devices height and interest are given to the composition.

Our trophy reminds us that being a winner--either in sports or reading--brings its own rewards.

Which is exactly what we can accomplish with good, creative displays.

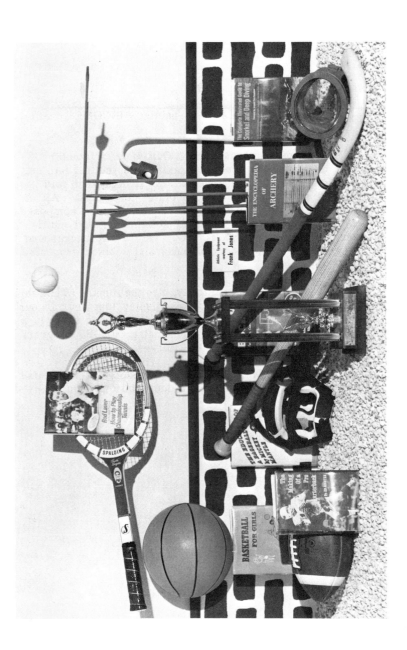

T plus AX equals TAX; namely, INCOME

The rebus helps us here. Our metal T combined with our ax spells out the word tax. This, cutting into our gilded log representing income, allows a deluge of gold coins--only gold foil covered chocolate--to escape. All of this happens against a background of skyscrapers composed of stock trading reports, financial statements, and multitudinous tax forms and books. Our yellow sky background dotted with a few television antennas and a black drop cloth complete the picture.

March and April, naturally, are the months to use this gentle reminder. Having used this display last year in our library I saved the necessary objects and reused them in a local bank along with a poster announcing our IRS program on income tax to be given at the library.

Sorry! You won't find any tax deductions with this one. There are no expenses nor depreciations entailed.

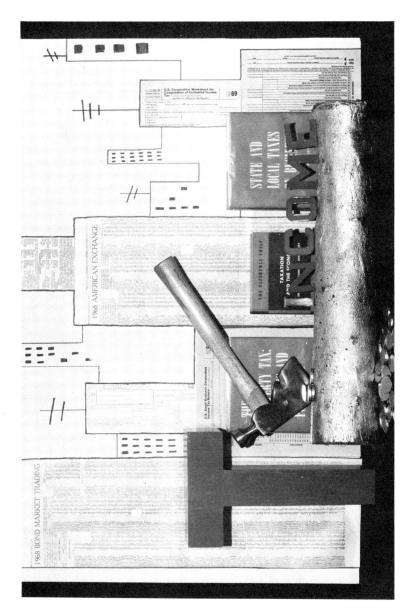

Carnival of Flowers

The theme has been provided by the local garden club. It remains for us to execute the idea in material form. For anyone who has been to a carnival or circus the ideas cannot be held back. Barkers, party hats, candy cotton, ice cream, pop corn, multi-colored leis, and prizes, prizes, prizes for everyone permeate the carnival atmosphere.

And we have included just about everything in this wonderfully, bizarrely colorful conglomeration. Even a snake charmer appearing in the picture couldn't add anything more. Since flowers are the main feature, we use flower pots for our people. Our foam faces are decorated with acetate sunglasses, party hats, artificial flowers and miscellaneous notions from the nearby novelty shop.

The presence of three darts on the backboard suggests that a winner of our game of chance--balloon breaking--will be the recipient of a prize shown (library leaflets and materials) in the smaller pots.

When the display was removed from our display window to the flower show site, where it was a prize winner, pop corn for passersby to munch was held in the end pots.

"All right, ladies and gentlemen, step right up. The show is just about to begin."

And it's your show, so get busy!

Hang Ups

Here, a currently popular word is used; a literal and figurative interpretation of a hip word now in vogue. The coat checks on each hanger relay this message.

EVERYONE	HAS	HANG UPS...
1	2	3

TRY	OURS.
4	5

NOW
6

Our nearest coat closet is the source of the six hangers which are painted Mandarin Red. The two wooden poles are painted black and the coat checks are printed in the aforementioned red. All of this against a stark white background provides a striking display.

In this particular instance books of a psychological and/or sociological nature are used but many varieties of subjects would be appropriate. Your subject is dependent upon the audience you are trying to reach.

Here is a very uncomplicated but effective way to make your point--and your display.

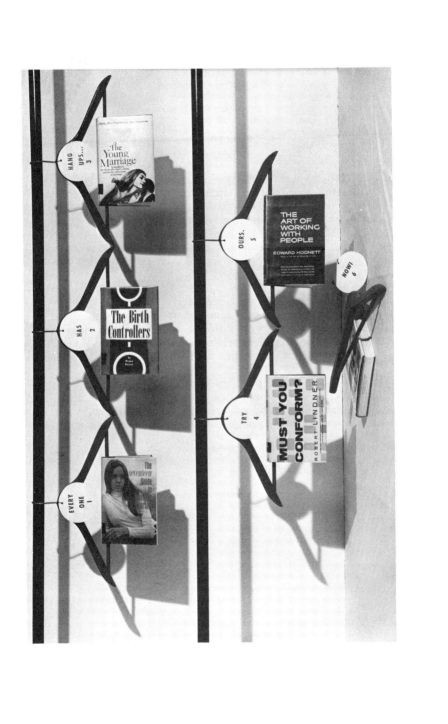

Mondrian

This display gives you a chance to plagiarize the famous painter Mondrian but in a different medium from his. Where he used oils to create his compositions, we use colored acetates and black matte tape on our glass front display area. These richly colored acetates with light shining through them from behind give us a brilliant Mondrian cópy.

Our art work in the background is from our circulating collection available to the public. The three dimensional letters spelling ART were salvaged from the front of our building when our merger with the county library necessitated our name change from Norristown Public Library. (In fact, all of these letters are being held for future use.)

We have developed two planes of interest each of which enhance the other without interference. The back portion is quite visible and can readily be seen through the lighter areas in front specifically included for this purpose.

OR . . .

Modern Cathedral Window

. . . as a contemporary church window our Mondrian "painting" acquires another aspect. Merely by changing the objects in the display we have created a completely different feeling and presented new ideas to our public.

The carved figures are borrowed from a neighborhood shop and we have, again, not delved into any of our budget funds.

Catholic Book Week or Easter are appropriate times for using this idea, or if a church group would be interested they could incorporate our display into their activities.

If time is ever lacking (which I hope will be rare) it is a good idea to have such a display on hand to insert rather than let another display on view become stale. New and changing exhibits keep your public interested.

14

Looking for Ideas?

Our friend Snoopy has momentarily taken time off from his many adventures to decorate his home and aid us in our promotion on interior designing. Before attempting his huge undertaking he peruses some of the books available on the subject; namely, Elegant Decorating On a Limited Budget by Janet Reist.

Working with Charles Schultz's format of a comic strip in mind, we try to create as one dimensional a display as possible. The white backdrop with black cardboard strips that outline the house and fence rails repeat the colors of our plastic friend. Only the books bring color into the display. We have achieved our comic strip frame and enhanced the books used.

Incorporating the books as part of the fence blends them into the overall picture. They are prominent but well integrated. When possible let your books serve a twofold purpose: here they promote the subject--which is only one of many that could be used--and act as fence uprights.

This display is also excellent for a bulletin board. By using the book jackets sans books and a paper cutout of Snoopy you have a perfect frame.

What will you or Snoopy think of next?

15

Dug Up Any Good Books Lately?

Finally our tombstone from Design 3 has appeared. Peering into our setting through our angel hair "cobwebs" we see a miniature pick ax leaning against our prized tombstone on which is scratched our question: "Dug Up Any Good Books Lately?" And in another part of our moss-covered, green crepe paper cavern two eyeballs peer back. Only the rubber spider seems calm and at home with the whole situation.

A simple, but effectively executed, Halloween theme that doesn't fall back on the hackeyed traditional materials. We've broken out of our rut for one holiday. Now why not try it with some of the others?

You know it can be done!

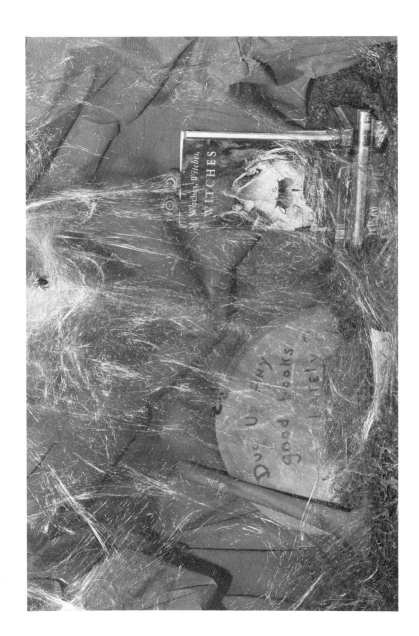

16

The Pause That

The Adult Education Program at your high school deserves your attention and an appropriate exhibition with some flair. How do you tell adults to go back to school? What message might reach them? What presentation will make them consider an evening class?

Thinking back to the approximate time when your to-be-reached audience was in school you research information on what was popular during their heyday. One of the things that has remained constant in the eye of the American public is Coca-Cola. So our American Fountain of Youth, Coke, becomes a means by which to reach not just one generation, but many.

A few reprints of ads (supplied by the Coca-Cola Company) from years gone by, some empty coke bottles (we borrowed ours from Miss Spring's Soda Emporium), a few bent straws and the list of evening classes available give you the illustrated presentation. Divided in half visually our exhibit is formed into a complete whole with our caption:

You've had "the pause that refreshes".

Now try the refreshers that stop pauses!

Now Drink up!

The pause that refreshes
Coca-Cola
Another OLD FAITHFUL–
pause that refreshes
with ice-cold Coca-Cola
Norristown Area School District
1968 ADULT EVENING SCHOOL
REGISTRATION
JANUARY 6-7-9-13-14-16
7 TO 9 P.M.
★ REGISTRATION INSTRUCTIONS... ★
★ SELECT YOUR COURSE and ENROLL TODAY ★
Norristown Area School District
1968 ADULT EVENING SCHOOL
THE NEW WORLD OF MATH
GERMAN
BRUSH UP YOUR FRENCH
Flower Arrangem
YOU'VE HAD "the pause that refreshes"
NOW TRY the refreshers that stop pauses!

17

Election Year

The New York Times practically did this entire display. The only problem involved is that it took them sixty-eight years to complete it!

Seventeen front pages announcing the national election results for the past sixty-eight years were supplied to us by the above newspaper. By mounting these on a board and trimming it with blue and red ribbon a perfect background was easily achieved. The various campaign buttons were obtained from a private collector in town. The rest of the items are from our permanent collection of miscellaneous gatherings.

Oh, yes--the face behind the 1968 is that of President Nixon.

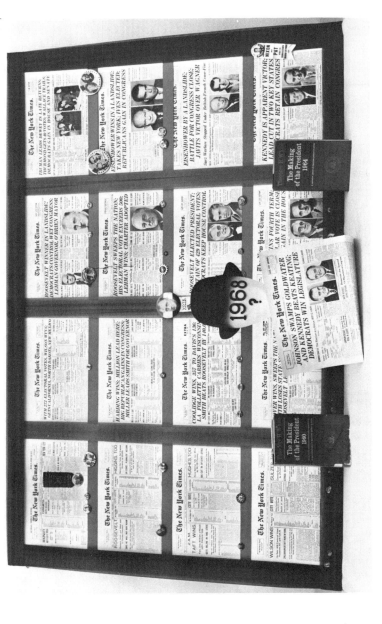

18

Quiet Please!
Mind Under Construction

When that shipping crate arrived from my brother in Japan, I knew it would someday be incorporated into a display. So with great care each piece was carefully removed and stored away.

National Children's Book Week approached. Out came the cherished boards. Construction was commenced. The large photograph blow up of the young boy reading was placed in position and piles and piles of books were heaped between the picture and the construction fence.

The materials alone in this display would not have conveyed our message. The entire display is pulled together by our caption: this is the catalyst that fused the other fragments into a solid statement.

Quiet Please! Next construction coming up.

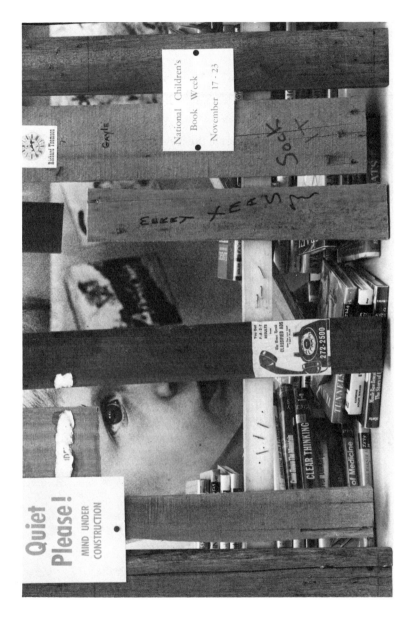

19

B awl U Can b. Read

Calling upon our friend the rebus once more we are able to effect a different interpretation of the slogan used for National Library Week. Translated from the above hieroglyphics the original slogan reads "Be all you can be. Read." Our display is the Rebus Version.

There certainly is very little expense involved here but we have been able to create a novelty which carries our national slogan. Instead of merely using the attractive posters provided for this occasion--they were used elsewhere on bulletin boards--we gather our inexpensive materials together and by using our imaginations have a display which pleases all.

Simple but effective. Materially inexpensive but rich in content.

B awl U can b. Design those displays!

20

Again, Be All You Can Be

National Library Week again offers another possibility for using an idea that is applicable to many displays with various themes.

The featured pictures are all borrowed from our friendly antique dealer. On each picture a caption balloon has been taped which reads, "Be all you can be. Read." Everyone seems to have one thought in mind. Here a touch of humor is interjected into our eternal message.

Imagine some of the many captions that could be used in place of this historic slogan:

"When did you last visit your library?"

"Have you read Portnoy's Complaint, yet?"

"I think your library books are overdue."

"Don't be a schnook. Read a book."

As a wall grouping, display case item, or as single pictures this idea provides a humorous means by which you can promote your theme.

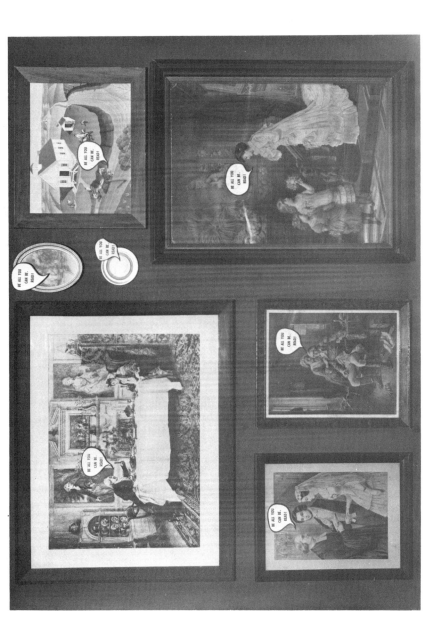

21

Happy Harvesting

Granny is out raking the leaves without which autumn is not complete. As one or two leaves still drift from above (with the aid of our nearly invisible nylon thread) she pauses to look up at the children hurrying off to their first days back at school. And, as we can see, for all those who read her already-gathered books (or any of those available) she promises a bountiful and happy harvest--which is exactly what reading provides.

Simple? Effective? Better than the Back to School signs seen everywhere at this time of year?

The rake and winter wheat are the only minor expenses involved for us. The basket is donated by the local market and stained a pumpkin orange. The yellow burlap and leaves are part of a commercial display previously donated.

And your cache--budget funds--are still yours. At this spending rate it promises to also be a bountiful winter.

22

A Pinch of This

Gourmands--gourmets and novices alike--are instantly drawn to our colorful larder where one can almost smell fresh bread baking or homemade vegetable soup simmering on the back burner. It is an enticement to try some of the many recipes available here and to search out the other new cookbooks still remaining in your collection.

Fruits and vegetables (artificial and borrowed from the local florist) add a dash of color; spices, fresh eggs and noodles add a pinch of authenticity; cooking implements stir in a measure of the days of yore. Bright yellow burlap and a wood-grained counter provide a warm and cheerful background.

Here is where you can turn to yourself and your own kitchen to find the materials needed for such a display. Everyone can certainly provide some basic equipment right from his own home.

What an inducement to pass by the frozen dinners and ready-mix sections the next time you shop at the supermarket!

23

American History

From the ashes and debris of the riots and internal conflicts that are going on in our country today, history is gathering material for its written records. American history now, moreso than ever, is recording the story of the black man in this country along with that of his white counterparts, and the two histories are becoming one in our country's chronicle.

The background is a piece of multicolored terry cloth on which cutouts from Look magazine have been pinned to form a montage. Appropriate books line the foreground.

A very direct message can be created by your display when words are used with a different connotation.

Who, during his academic career, has not taken a course in American history?

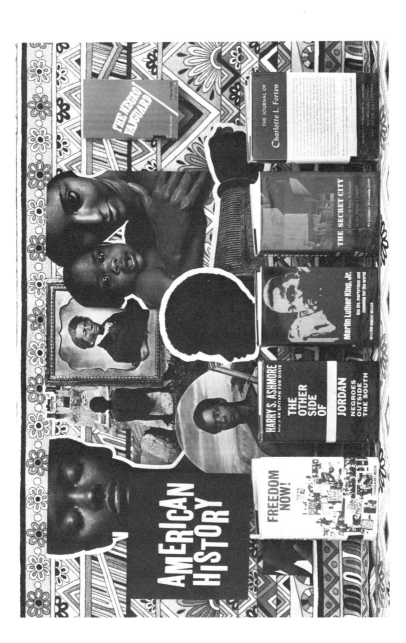

24

Printing Perspective

The apex of our black and white checkerboard trapezoid is rounded off with a minute copy of John White Alexander's The Pictograph (the original is one of six murals in the Library of Congress). The books on printing are surrounded by printing letters which read backwards spell various words used by the profession. The total effect is a concise perspective of printing.

By using a strong, geometric background you create a forceful backdrop for your subject matter. Here, black and white is used to further the basic ideas associated with printing.

This particular setting can easily be used for other ideas that appeal to you and can provide a background for numerous events.

The expense is nil. Use your standard backdrop, gather a few materials that are strong in composition to compete with your background, add your books and you will have everything in fine perspective.

25

Christmastide

Deck the Halls--and that is just what everyone seems to do during this season. In fact, from Thanksgiving until the end of each year Christmas decorations flourish. Perhaps a little too much so, so why not try serenity and meaningfulness as a basis for a display?

Here, a quiet Madonna surrounded by three silver angels against a green flock background dominates the view through a cutout cross of plywood painted white with green trim. St. Matthew, Chapter Two is the passage to which the Bible is opened. The white rose is used to bring to mind the fable of The Legend of the Christmas Rose by Selma Lagerlöf.

This display creates a pleasant pause in the frenzied shopping and festivities which accompany this time of the year and keeps all of your materials--for which there is a great demand--available for circulation.

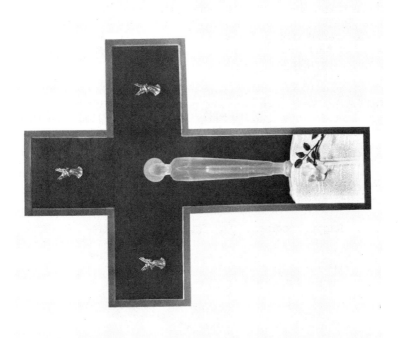

26

Time to Fly With Books

Zooming across our smiling sun the Spirit of Mont-Norris* proclaims with its banner that it is Time to Fly With Books. Books on wings of colored acetate lazily circle around waiting for us to climb aboard and travel with them, if only vicariously. Our pâpier-maché sun radiates against a bright, yellow sky.

This display is a great idea to use after the festive End-of-the-Year holidays have passed and the Winter Doldrums of January and February have set in. This is a time of year when we all need a lift as we pay our bills, and await Spring's arrival.

And for those who plan an actual vacation, what could be better preparation than a bit of reading beforehand of the places to be visited?

Happy Landings!

*Montgomery County-Norristown
Public Library

27

Mirror, Mirror

Like Noah's dove our feathered friend brings us a message--"If Winter comes, can Spring be far behind?"*-- and surveys the slow changing terrain from his lofty perch. Below, a few patches of grass and three croci brave the lingering snows to herald the approach of Spring. Trees of mirror and green stand sentinel as our transition transpires.

Before the earth blooms forth again there is a slow awakening process which is captured here along with the promise of Spring's rebirth.

Artificial snow, grass and croci snuggle in among the mirrors which have been cut and painted to represent ever-greens. A modest investment obtained the materials for this display which will lend itself to many more uses in the coming months.

But, for the moment, our transition piece is complete and gives us a chance to reflect on our coming plans and displays.

*Shelley's "Ode to the West Wind."

28

Pick-a-Direction

Rockets, labeled with the names of various professions, roar by in all directions. Two cutouts of the modern youth of today ponder their decisions in the background. Our space-ship, Pick-a-Direction, blasts off. American Education Week is in orbit.

In this fast-paced world we can hopefully aid these youths in selecting a vocation. Books on various careers abound, and our purpose in this display is to create an interest in one or more of the vocational fields.

Colored construction paper cut from patterns drawn freehand provides our busts. A roll of knitting yarn provides our tracer tracks for the printed rockets. Vivid hues of red, orange, green, yellow, purple, and blue are used in keeping with the color-crazed artwork of today. Pin letters painted a bright red announce the specific occasion.

Education costs may be rising but our display expenses certainly are not!

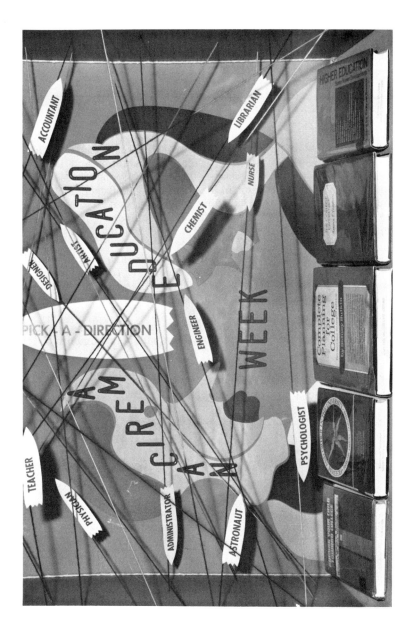

29

Cities

Against a skyscraper background of newspaper articles pertaining to cities our book "buildings" stand, each in its own landscaped block of real estate ads. Sponge trees and shrubbery adorn the terrain. A mirror foundation is the highlight of the center "building". (When this display was torn down, three pennies were found. Someone obviously made his three wishes.)

The only requirements needed here are an old newspaper or two, scissors, glue, patience and a little time. Even the ability to draw a straight line need not be present-- a good ruler makes a fine substitution.

It's surprising how many articles seem to be available on a particular subject when the newspaper is carefully scanned.

You even stand a chance of a profit with this display if you include a fountain for wishing.

30

Outer City

What community does not have its problems?

Problems are not confined to one community: they prevail everywhere. Our library's booklist--The Outer City--which lists some of the reading materials available on this subject, is the basis for our display.

The map (cut in outline form) of Montgomery County was obtained from our County Commissioners. The houses are simple to construct--two models are cut from a decorating magazine and duplicates are made on a Xerox machine. Cardboard lighting, paste-on letters and the two booklists complete our community project. Books listed are set aside at the circulation desk along with additional copies of The Outer City.

This inexpensive project reverts to our cut out and paste method but still puts our message across. A bulletin board also lends itself very nicely to this method.

With aids like this, fair weather is forecast for better living conditions everywhere.

31

P. T. A.

The school bell has rung. Parents gather for the monthly meeting of the P. T. A. The thatched schoolhouse stands in readiness to house the complaints and accolades all parents harbor with school systems and their children. But with Widow Johnson approaching the meeting this certainly promises to be a P. T. A. meeting of a different nature.

A slight departure from book displays for the moment and we turn our attention to records and obviously a song of great popularity--Harper Valley P. T. A. The record itself shines in the sky. The path leading up to the school is a collection of record album cover replicas cut from a magazine ad. The parents are loaned by a fellow employee and are made of dried apples and nuts; Mrs. Johnson is a modern innovation.

Our "hip" set really approves of this one and another of our services has been brought to our public's attention. Imagine what possibilities the rest of your record collection offers.

Swing to it!

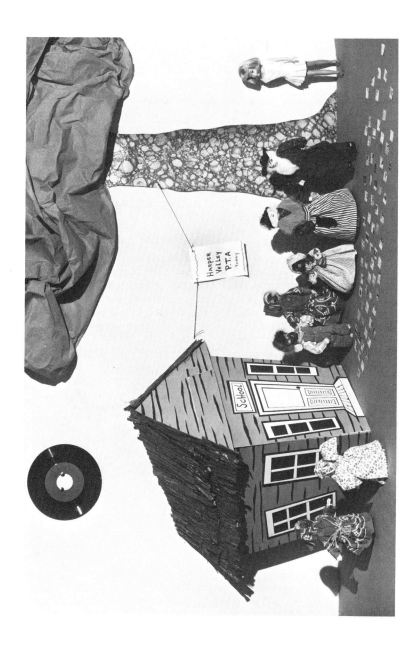

32

Blackboard Jungle

There are times when school seems to be just one maze after another--a jungle of assignments, problems, essays, etc. To guide one through this jungle we offer our help by providing books. And we certainly can provide plenty of these at our various outposts.

Here is another example where no cost has been incurred. All of the materials shown were already available and merely needed assembling. Our blackboard was borrowed from its practical day-to-day functions; the three R's again came from the salvaged letters mentioned in Design Twelve; imagination required a small amount of time to develop the theme.

Class is in session. Time for roll call of all your materials and ideas. Prepare your course, apply the necessary study, and then plan to graduate magna cum laude with your displays. As with any chosen curriculum, your best efforts are needed to come through with top honors.

Report Cards Friday

TUES:

BLACKBOARD JUNGLE

Spanish II translate pp 71-77

Browning's ___ in a year

Ovid and Virgil p. 367

Cybernetics pp. 28-36

Due Thursday $\frac{N}{2} = 1.92 = x$

Ch 9 — Waverley Novels

$4AL + 3O_2 \rightarrow 2ALO_3$

Dryden and the tragedy and the heroic play

p. 135 Language and Reality

The Latin ___

Test: Ch. 3-10 Monday

$A^2 + B^2 = C^2$

? = C

RR Galileo

Measurement

Algebra Exam Friday

Book R___

33

Stuck in a Blind?

Visit your library!

Our duckling seems perplexed, momentarily.
Fortunately, this blind is Venetian and not one used by
hunters. A blind can also be lack of understanding or judg-
ment, so a visit to the library can alleviate this condition.

Our pun has made its point and our display.

The materials used are readily accessible to everyone. The Venetian blind is borrowed from a local household
goods supplier, the duck was purchased for a few pennies at
the toy store, and the sand and wheat were gathered during
one of many sources and supplies excursions.

So don't remain in any kind of a blind yourself. Keep
scouring for supplies and have them available when ideas
like this need materializing.

34

Easter Promenade

High society vies for attention with the magnificent floral arrangements bordering the background. Our rabbit couturier beams approvingly as he surveys his masterpieces in this huge, Easter basketlike creation. His pièce de résistance is the framed, original jacket design for The Egg Tree created (and presented to our library) by Katherine Milhous. When has there been a finer assemblage for an Easter Promenade?

The materials are self-evident: artificial flowers, colored cellophane straw, foam eggs decorated with bits of fabric and jewelry, and, in this particular display, the generous donation of Katherine Milhous. Our floral pieces are created and on loan from a local florist who has been given the proper credit. A piece of turquoise felt completes the setting.

On with your hats, please. The judges--your public --await your next creation.

35

Picket

Another riot in the making! Everyone is actively fighting for his cause these days and Brands X, Y and Z are no exception. But the materials plastered over the fence dominate the scene.

Through the subversive efforts of the American Cancer Society our pack of picketers seem to be diminishing and no longer form the same binding chain: they are becoming the butt of our distaste. Our sentinel, <u>Smoking and Health</u> by the U. S. Dept. of Health, stands by to prevent any further destructiveness. Who knows? Our picketers' plans may all go up in smoke someday.

The fence previously used in Design 18 as foreground has now become the background and has several posters provided by the ACS pasted to it. The artificial grass provides a good backing for our picketers who are . . . .

Sorry, no discriminating.

36

Sow

Spring brings with its arrival many rewards.
Thoughts of gardening is one. Our seeds, bulbs, pots and
green grass throw us right into the spirit of this annual
event; a pair of gardening gloves offer a silent prayer for
the coming season; brightly colored parasols add to the
festive atmosphere.   Even our romantic doves convey
Spring's eternal message of rebirth.

This seasonal display brightens our viewers'
thoughts.   Working hand-in-hand with the seed catalogs
that are filling the mails at this time of the year we en-
courage the use of our many books on the subject of
gardening--whether it be flower or vegetable.

Hopefully our lovebirds will not thwart our expecta-
tions and someday will return with their offspring to ad-
mire the rewards of our labors of love.

So, sow!--this idea and many more of your own
grafting.

37

For a Better Look at Your Own World . . .

Messages flash from earth. For a better look at
your own world . . . for a better look . . . . So our
space team investigates one of the world atlases available
on the subject. In the meantime three outer space
creatures stare in awe at what must seem a gigantic
monster to them--earth.

Space, a timely topic, is the nucleus around which
is constructed our theme of informative sources regarding
our own planet. Our space men and creatures actually
came from the toy store. White snow paper against a
dark blue ground and one world globe complete our picture.

Hopefully, our space creatures are friendly.

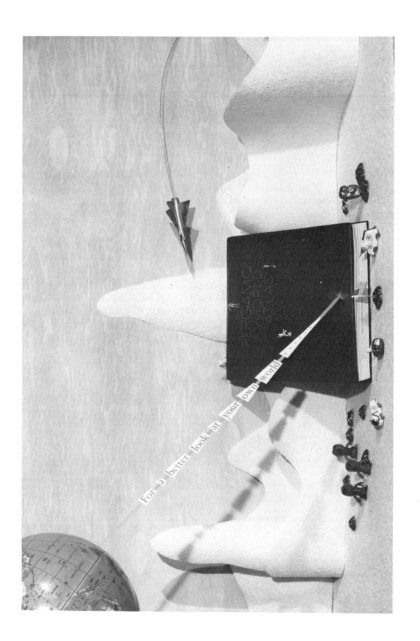

PERGAMON WORLD ATLAS

For a better look at your own world!

38

Be Kind

Such pleading eyes look up at us from behind bars. Everyone wants a home and our imprisoned friends are no exception. Who has ever visited a kennel or pound and not experienced the fervent desire to unlock all of the cage doors and take everyone home?

Our Be Kind to Animals Week display captures the interest of all passersby. No age is immune to a cuddly pet even if he is just on loan from the local novelty store.

The bars are heavy dowels painted a bright yellow. A piece of wallpaper lines the floor. Our animal drawings are borrowed from a young artist--age 9--whose interest in animals is apparent. And our courtesy cards are included in appreciation of both loans.

There was consideration given to the idea of using the sign "Do Not Feed the Animals," but that would not be kind.

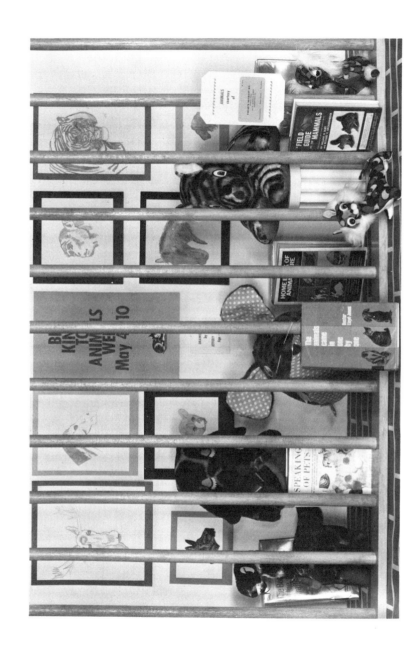

39

Firm Foundations

If you have built castles in the air, your
work need not be lost; that is where they
should be. Now put the foundations under
them.

Thoreau

Slowly we build our foundation upon which our castles
will rest and remain secure. Our building bricks are
books; our trowel a library card. Our clouds drift by.
One contains the above quotation. Our statement and display are complete.

So very often a display can be built around a quotation or verse (e. g. , Design 6) and illustrated in such a way
that it is given new meaning. Certainly Thoreau did not
have this illustration in mind when he created these sen-
tences nearly a hundred years ago. But he has aided us in
our display and we, hopefully, have been a credit to his
work.

40

A Word to the Wise

Our conclave of owls and owlets convene in their shady glade to possibly elect a new leader or perhaps to learn more of their heritage. As in any coed gathering there are bound to be one or two young blades who have a wandering eye or flirtatious wink for a coy maiden. It is suspected that our tiniest friend nestling in the overhanging branches may not have been invited and obviously has escaped detection by our eagle-eyed proctor.

Regardless of their purpose (for which we can all find our own interpretation) their very presence gives us our display.

Pine boughs and needles, a generous collector's owl symposium, and a little imagination--with the help of nylon cord to suspend the branches--give us a tranquil but enticing scene.

I hope these words to the wise are sufficient enough to provoke additional ideas in you.

41

Art Nouveau

Quite often the simplest combination of materials can express your ideas provided the materials are exactly right. Here, only one book is used; the entire display is built around the title and subject matter--<u>The Flowering of Art Nouveau</u>.

One statuette of this period illustrates the title and captures the feeling we want to prevail. The fabric background of a gold, orange, green and purple design further enhances our topic. Our floral fan of carved ivory balances and completes the setting. Just the right pieces are combined. Careful, but certainly not elaborate, planning is the prime requisite.

Any additional material would create confusion. The book jacket design and flowing print background provide enough line and color. Even though this particular era was of very ornate design we do not want to overdo our display lest it obscure our subject matter.

Simplicity can be effective.

42

Alice

"Feel like <u>Alice In Wonderland</u> when in the library?
Ask our reference librarian for assistance."

So reads the sign on the top book shelf while below,
Alice tries in vain to reach the tiny key on the glass table.

Here, more attention is paid to detail and the results show. Plenty of time must be allowed for a display
of this nature. There is no hurrying such a project.

Our antique dealer came through with just the right
suite of furniture for Alice's room. (Courtesy card on the
top shelf also.) The wallpaper is pink and white mattress
ticking above a painted chair rail. The rug is a deep pink
print fabric which was a remnant at our local mill-end
shop. The accessories throughout the room were loaned by
a fellow employee.

This is the same display case used for the other
exhibits but it has been divided by a frosted glass ceiling
which keeps the room in scale, supports the overhead book-
shelf and allows light to filter through. What started out as
a simple project turned into a very detailed but rewarding
display.

Remember, this really takes time, so be prepared.
And also be prepared for many, many compliments. This
is the type of display people don't want to leave because
there is so much to see. They love it and so do you!

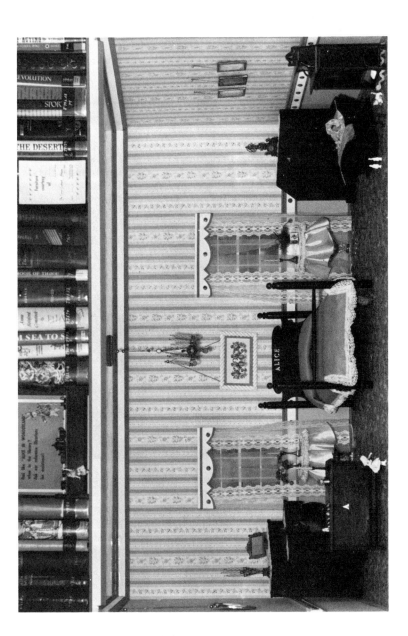

43

Variations

The photographs that appear in this book show one use of each display. In some of the text describing these displays other ideas have been listed. Still more possibilities exist and the following ideas expound a few of these. To this list you can (and will) add your own. Remember, this book is only the first step of many to be taken. The numbers refer to the designs previously discussed.

-6-

Our den atmosphere lends itself nicely to such captions as "An Antidote for TV," "Restful Moments," or "A Study for Good Studying."

-9-

The rebus is fun and offers many chances to combine objects to form words as we did in Design 19. Use a few of the other titles in this book such as "Blackboard Jungle" or "Pick-a-Direction" to start practicing.

-14-

Snoopy is always willing to join in with a good idea. There is no limit on the topics he could be perusing in front of his doghouse. Anything from ice skating to flying to the moon is his forte.

-20-

Any number of pictures could be used in this type of arrangement with almost any balloon caption you would like. The other captions listed in the chapter are but a minute selection.

-24-

This background can be used for many displays of various subject matter. Or think of it as a checkerboard with the caption "Your Move" attached to it.

-25-

The cross shown here can be used for an Easter setting, Memorial Day display, or any religious occasion around which you plan a theme.

-27-

Christmas, winter sports, and outer space are just three other uses these abstract forms have filled. Their design could be that of trees or mountains; the accessories with them will determine their interpretation.

-29-

This Design and Design 19 utilize subject-related newspaper clippings as background buildings. Wherever you can use a city skyline, just clip articles pertaining to your subject and build.

-31-

School functions and activities are great for this one but please keep the Widow Johnson home if you want to accomplish any official business.

-40-

Wisdom, owls and knowledge are synonymous. This might even be a meeting of librarians or a lodge convention. Appropriate materials and labeling is all that is needed to give our gathering definition.

    With a few minor changes this could be any room
and could serve as a display for decorating, antique furniture, doll collecting, etc. With detailed work such as
this, be certain you keep all the pieces after it has been
taken down. You can use it again--as is, or with a fresh
coat of paint--when it will seem new to your public's eye.

44

Do--Don't

Don't disregard your own ideas regardless of how "out" or inconsequential they may seem. Keep a notebook for Everyday and Fantastic Ideas. If something is not feasible at the moment, perhaps next month or next year it will be. Remember, flying to the moon was yesteryear's dream achieved only by Flash Gordon and Buck Rogers; today it's our reality.

Do avoid useless captions. Let the subject matter speak for itself when possible. If your display's theme is winter, Easter or gardening, you don't always need a big label stating such. In some instances, and I know the tar pots will be put on to boil, "one picture IS worth . . . ." If you have done your job well there will be no need to tell your public what you have done. They will know.

Do consider the possibility of building your displays around a slogan, clever caption or apt phrase. The possibility of starting with the cart in lieu of the horse sometimes works to your advantage. Here is where our notebook aids us in retaining any particular jingles or wordings that cross our minds or come to our attention. Write them down.

Do watch the budget. This, of course, is obligatory. Save on expenses whenever possible but when there is a choice in quality try to select the best possible. If, for example, you need to purchase a figure or objet d'art, etc., and the one that costs a few cents or dollars more will enhance your work to better advantage, use it. You will find other ways to save.

Don't keep using and reusing the same materials for any excessively long periods of time. Sometimes a part or parts of a display are worth keeping only if they can be used in an entirely different concept. Materials should be fresh and constantly updated.

Do maintain your enthusiasm. There will be times when everything will seem wrong and you couldn't care less about displaying for the local garden club. This is the time to forget the entire subject--momentarily. Take a rest. Then come back. Every hour of the day is not going to produce a brilliant idea for you. But they will crop up at the oddest times: while watching television, having dinner, or perhaps while out shopping. (Get out that notebook.) Chances are that you will be working alone in your endeavors. There may not be too much moral support when you are in need. Make your own. You can!

Don't limit your source of supplies and materials. Constantly search for new sources. Approach many and varied shops as possible suppliers. Letters or telephone calls to various individuals, firms, organizations, or clubs often provide bountiful results. And never forget nature's unlimited supplies. Seek and find.

Do record your work. Take pictures, keep a scrap-book, or folder, with complete information as to what you have accomplished. Slides can be an excellent means to keep track of the good work you have done. Review your work. Look for the bad as well as the good features so your projects will continue to improve. With constant practice you will be amazed and pleased with the great strides forward you have achieved. Who knows? You may be on your way to your own book on displays.

Now, have fun!

Appreciation Appendix

Alice's furniture	The Corner Cupboard
Animal drawings	Jeffery Feist--Age 9
Antique pictures	Nancy's Antique Shop
Athletic equipment	Frank Jones Sporting Goods
Campaign buttons	Ray Butera
Caricature	Mr. Marcus
Election results	New York Times
Encouragement	Joan Sinclair
Floral arrangements	Mary Catanese Florist
Nut and apple dolls	Marge Owens
Owl collection	Loy Hanna
Photographs	Chester E. Pancoast
Religious statuettes	The Catholic Shop
Snoopy	Charles Schultz
Tombstone	Norristown Memorials, Inc.
Toy animals	Oscar's Novelty Shop
Venetian blind	Frank Batdorf
Widow Johnson	Kimberly Feist
Will	Pearl Frankenfield
Yours truly	Mother
Zeal	Betty Rossotti

Index